READING POWER FOR MINECRAFTERS

Grades 1-2

FUN SKILL-BUILDING ACTIVITIES TO PRACTICE VOCABULARY, SIGHT WORDS, SENTENCE STRUCTURE, READING COMPREHENSION, AND MORE!

Caroline Bryan

Illustrated by Amanda Brack

Sky Pony Press

New York

Copyright © 2021 by Hollan Publishing, Inc.
Minecraft® is a registered trademark of Notch Development AB.

The Minecraft game is copyright © Mojang AB.

Sky Pony Press books may be purchased in bulk at special discounts for sales promotion, corporate gifts, fund-raising, or educational purposes. Special editions can also be created to specifications. For details, contact the Special Sales Department, Sky Pony Press, 307 West 36th Street, 11th Floor, New York, NY 10018 or info@skyhorsepublishing.com.

Sky Pony® is a registered trademark of Skyhorse Publishing, Inc.®, a Delaware corporation.

Minecraft® is a registered trademark of Notch Development AB. The Minecraft game is copyright © Mojang AB.

Visit our website at www.skyponypress.com.

10 9 8 7 6 5 4 3 2 1

Library of Congress Cataloging-in-Publication Data is available on file.

Print ISBN: 978-1-5107-6623-5

Book design by Noora Cox
Cover and interior illustrations by Amanda Brack

Printed in China

A NOTE TO PARENTS

When you want to reinforce classroom skills at home, it's crucial to have kid-friendly learning materials. This workbook transforms reading practice into an irresistible adventure complete with diamond swords, zombies, skeletons, and creepers. That means less arguing over homework and more fun overall.

Reading Power for Minecrafters: Grades 1–2 is also fully aligned with National Common Core Standards for 1st and 2nd English Language Arts (ELA). What does that mean, exactly? All of the problems in this book correspond to what your child is expected to learn in school. This eliminates confusion and builds confidence for greater homework-time success!

As the workbook progresses, the reading becomes more advanced. Encourage your child to progress at his or her own pace. Learning is best when students are challenged, but not frustrated. What's most important is that your Minecrafter is engaged in his or her own learning.

Whether it's the joy of seeing their favorite game characters on every page or the thrill of discovering new words, there is something in this workbook to entice even the most reluctant reader.

Happy adventuring!

SHORT A

*Draw a line to connect the picture with the **short a** word.*

1.

A. hat

2.

B. bat

3.

C. cat

4.

D. sat

5.

E. glass

SHORT A

*Finish each sentence with one of these **short a** words.*

hat	bat	cat	sat	glass

1. A _____ sleeps upside down on blocks.

2. You can tame a _____ by feeding it fish.

3. That creeper is wearing a _____ .

4. Fill a _____ bottle with water.

5. Alex _____ on a pig.

LONG A

*Draw a line to connect the picture with the **long a** word.*

1.

A. hay

2.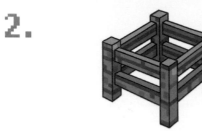

B. strays

3.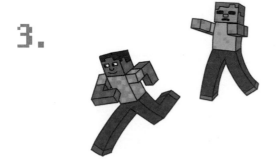

C. gate

4.

D. chase

5.

E. cave

LONG A

*Finish each sentence with one of these **long a** words.*

hay	strays	gate	chase	cave

1. Alex is lost in a _____ .

2. A _____ keeps the sheep inside the yard.

3. Zombies can _____ you into a house.

4. Horses eat _____ bales.

5. _____ are mobs that live in the cold.

SHORT E

*Draw a line to connect the picture with the **short e** word.*

1.

A. gems

2.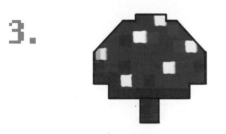

B. bed

3.

C. wet

4.

D. red

5.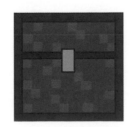

E. chest

8

SHORT E

*Finish each sentence with one of these **short e** words.*

gem	wet	bed	red	chest

1. A _____ can be carried by a llama.

2. An emerald is a rare _____ .

3. I found a _____ mushroom growing in a pot.

4. The ground is _____ .

5. Make a _____ with wool and wood planks.

LONG E

*Draw a line to connect the picture with the **long e** word.*

1.

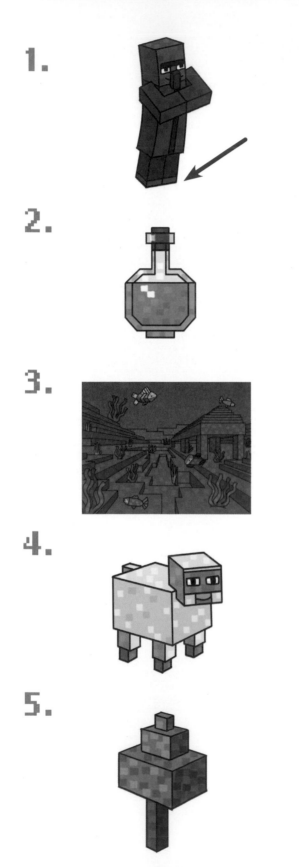

A. r**ee**f

2.

B. f**ee**t

3.

C. tr**ee**

4.

D. gr**ee**n

5.

E. sh**ee**p

LONG E

*Finish each sentence with one of these **long e** words.*

reef	feet	tree	green	sheep

1. A villager has two _____ .

2. A _____ potion lets you jump high.

3. A coral _____ grows in warm water.

4. You can dye the wool of a _____ .

5. Steve plants a tall _____ .

SHORT I

*Draw a line to connect the picture with the **short i** word.*

1.

A. lit

2.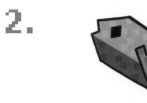

B. dig

3.

C. flip

4.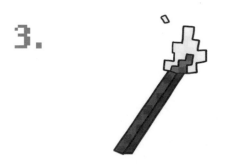

D. pig

5.

E. fish

SHORT I

*Finish each sentence with one of these **short i** words.*

lit	dig	flip	pig	fish

1. Steve used a pickaxe to _____ .

2. The cat ate a raw _____ .

3. I _____ the torch.

4. You can ride a _____ with a saddle.

5. Spiders _____ onto their backs when they die.

LONG I

*Draw a line to connect the picture with the **long i** word.*

1.

2.

3.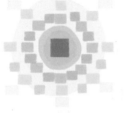

4.

5.

A. fire

B. mine

C. spider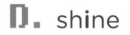

D. shine

E. time

LONG I

*Finish each sentence with one of these **long i** words.*

fire	mine	spider	shine	time

1. A Minecraft clock tells the _____ .

2. Keep away from _____ !

3. The sun can _____ all day.

4. A _____ can drop string.

5. Steve uses a pickaxe to _____ the block.

SHORT O

*Draw a line to connect the picture with the **short o** word.*

1.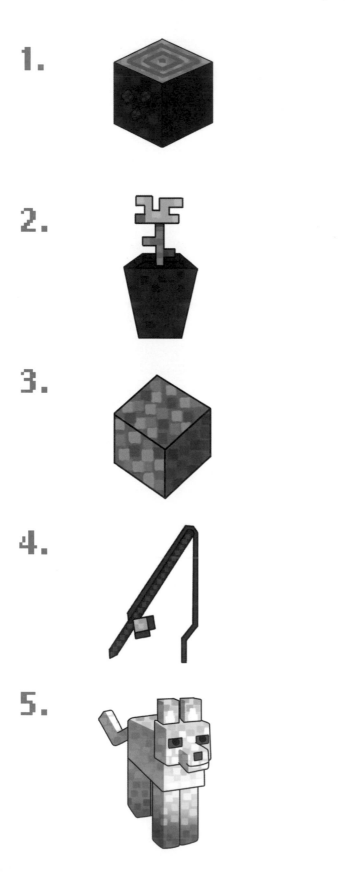

A. r**o**d

2.

B. l**o**g

3.

C. f**o**x

4.

D. p**o**t

5.

E. cobblestone bl**o**ck

SHORT O

*Finish each sentence with one of these **short o** words.*

rod	logs	fox	pot	block

1. Alex built a house with oak _____ .

2. You can grow a flower in a _____ .

3. The Enderman moved the cobblestone _____ .

4. Use a fishing _____ to reel in fish.

5. An arctic _____ hunts fish.

LONG O

*Draw a line to connect the picture with the **long o** word.*

1.

A. b**o**ne

2.

B. gr**o**w

3.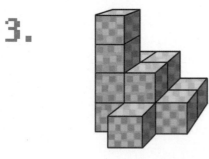

C. arr**o**w

4.

D. st**o**ne

5.

E. b**o**at

LONG O

*Finish each sentence with one of these **long o** words.*

bones	grow	arrow	stone	boat

1. An _____ can help you fight mobs.

2. A _____ axe is stronger than a wooden axe.

3. You row a _____ with paddles.

4. Plant a sapling to_____ a tree.

5. Skeletons drop _____ , bows, and arrows.

SHORT U

*Draw a line to connect the picture with the **short u** word.*

1.

A. hut

2.

B. cut

3.

C. sun

4.

D. buzz

5.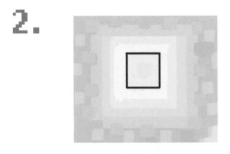

E. mud

SHORT U

*Finish each sentence with one of these **short u** words.*

hut	cut	sun	buzz	mud

1. I _____ wool and cobwebs with shears.

2. A swamp _____ is a small, square house.

3. Skeletons burn in the _____ .

4. A bee makes a _____ noise.

5. The dirty pig rolled in the _____ .

LONG U

*Draw a line to connect the picture with the **long u** word.*

1.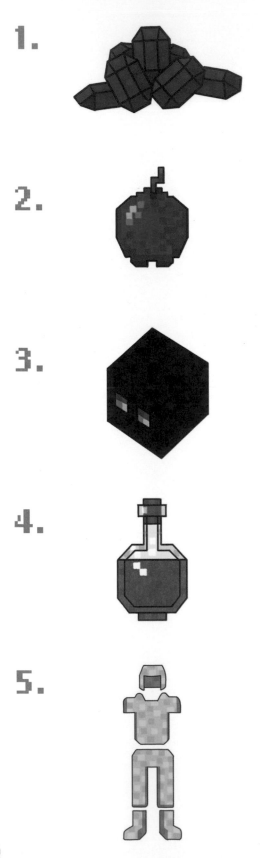

A. fruit

2.

B. suit

3.

C. blue

4.

D. rubies

5.

E. cube

LONG U

*Finish each sentence with one of these **long u** words.*

fruit	suit	blue	rubies	cube

1. _____ ice is found on the base of icebergs.

2. Steve put on a _____ of armor.

3. A Magma _____ has red, orange and yellow eyes.

4. The Golden apple is a rare _____ with healing power.

5. _____ are used to buy items in Minecraft Earth.

SENTENCE BUILDING WITH STEVE

A **subject** is the person, place, or thing that the sentence is about. A **predicate** is the part of the sentence that tells about the **subject**. It contains the **verb** (the action word).

Connect the subject of the sentence with the predicate. The first one is done for you.

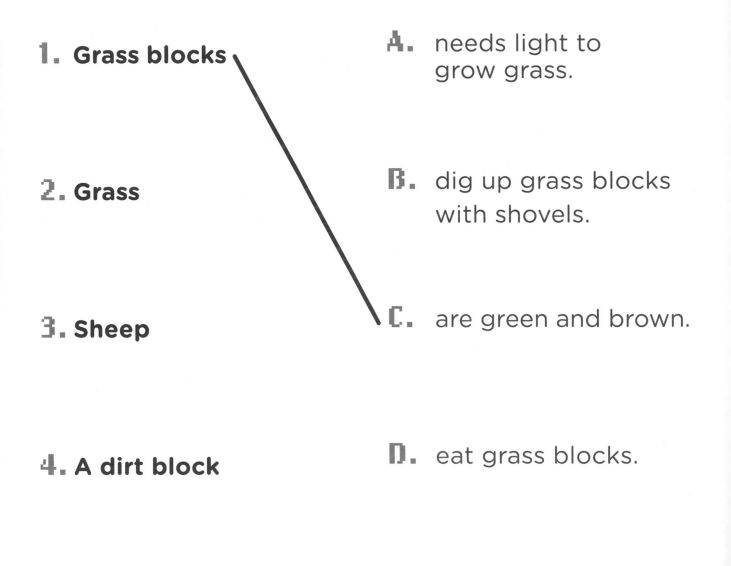

1. **Grass blocks**

2. **Grass**

3. **Sheep**

4. **A dirt block**

5. **Players**

A. needs light to grow grass.

B. dig up grass blocks with shovels.

C. are green and brown.

D. eat grass blocks.

E. grows in sunlight.

PARTS OF A SENTENCE

Read the sentences out loud. Then, mark each part of the sentence. The first one is done for you.

- Circle the first **noun** (person, place, or thing).

- Underline the **verb**.

1. (Piglins) <u>live</u> in the Nether.

2. They like gold armor.

3. Lava hurts them.

4. Baby piglins are passive mobs.

5. A piglin becomes a zombie in the Overworld.

MEET ZOMBIFIED PIGLINS

There are three ways a zombified piglin is made.

First, it can spawn in the crimson forest. Second, it

can appear when a pig gets hit by lightning. Finally,

a piglin that walks into the Overworld becomes a

zombified piglin. It only takes 15 seconds for the

piglin to turn into a zombie!

List the three ways a zombified piglin is made:

1. It can spawn in the _____ .

2. It can appear when a pig gets _____

by lightning.

3. A piglin that walks into the _____

becomes a zombified piglin.

ALEX AND THE LOOT CHEST

Read about Alex and the chest. Then answer the questions on the next page.

Alex runs to the chest. She is very fast. What will she find? Alex uses a pickaxe to open the chest. Wow! She found five gold bars. She will use the gold bars, or ingots, to make strong tools!

1. Alex is very

    ☐ slow   ☐ fast   ☐ loud

2. What does Alex find in the chest?

    ☐ **diamond blocks**

    ☐ **gold bars**

    ☐ **grass blocks**

3. How many bars does Alex find in the chest?

    ☐ three   ☐ five   ☐ nine

4. What will Alex make with the blocks she found?

    ☐ stew   ☐ string   ☐ tools

HOW TO TAME A LLAMA

Read about a llama. Then connect the phrases in the left column with the correct answers in the right column.

Before you tame a llama, it is wild. A wild llama can throw you to the ground. You have to ride the llama many times to tame it. When it is tame, you will see red hearts. You can put chests on the back of a tame llama. When you ride a llama, you cannot steer it. Walk with a llama on a lead or rope to steer it. Other llamas may follow!

1. A wild llama can

A. ride it.

2. You can place a chest

B. throw you to the ground.

3. To tame a llama, you should

C. when the llama is tame.

4. You will see red hearts

D. lead, or rope.

5. You can walk a llama on a

E. on a llama's back.

MEET MAGMA CUBES

Read about Magma Cubes. Then finish the statements and answer the question on the next page.

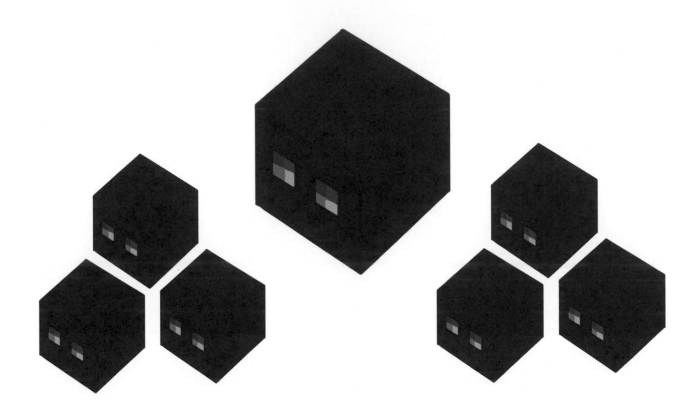

A magma cube hops around. It attacks by jumping onto a player. When a magma cube is killed, it breaks into smaller cubes. Large magma cubes are stronger and harder to fight than tiny magma cubes. Large cubes can jump 4 blocks high but tiny cubes can only jump 1 block high.

1. Magma cubes attack by _____ onto a player.

2. When a magma cube is killed it breaks into

    _____ .

3. Tiny magma cubes can only jump _____ block high.

4. List one reason that large magma cubes are more difficult to fight.

    _____

    _____

    _____

ABANDONED VILLAGES

Read about abandoned villages. Then check **true** *or* **false** *for the statements on the next page.*

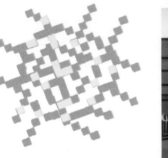

Abandoned villages are empty villages. They are dark and quiet and very dirty. They have no light or torches and no doors on the houses. Look on the ground to find mossy cobblestones and cobwebs. Stray cats with no homes wander the streets. Watch out! A zombie villager can appear in an empty village!

1. Abandoned villages are clean.

2. There are no doors on the houses of abandoned villages.

3. You can find mossy cobblestones on the ground there.

4. Pet cats live in the homes there.

5. Abandoned villages are dark because there are no light sources.

6. Abandoned villages are safe.

ALEX'S SNOWY WALK

Read about Alex's walk. Then circle the correct answer to the questions on the next page.

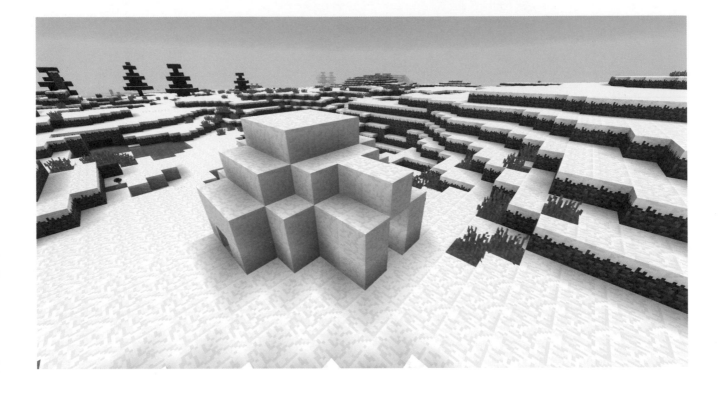

Alex is walking in the snow. She is cold and hungry. Look! Alex sees an igloo! She will be warm inside the igloo. First, she makes a fire using wood for fuel. Then, she heats rabbit stew to eat. Finally, she sleeps in a bed. Alex is happy she found an igloo!

1. Alex is walking in the

   A. swamp.

   B. snow.

   C. grass.

2. In the snow, Alex is feeling

   A. **cold and hungry.**

   B. **sick and hot.**

   C. **warm and sleepy.**

3. Inside the igloo, Alex makes a

   A. **book.**

   B. **coat.**

   C. **fire.**

4. Alex eats

   A. **rabbit stew.**

   B. **raw fish.**

   C. **red apple.**

5. Alex is _____ she found an igloo!

   A. sad

   B. happy

   C. confused

MEET STRAYS

Read about Strays. Then fill in the blanks on the next page.

Strays are skeletons that are

always found in cold places. They

fight with a bow and arrow. Did

you know a stray can ride on a spider?

This is called a stray spider jockey.

Strays drop bones and arrows

when they are killed.

1. Strays are found in _____ .

2. Strays fight with a _____ and _____ .

3. A stray spider jockey is a stray riding

   on a _____ .

4. A stray drops bones and arrows when

   it is _____ .

STEVE AND ALEX'S STUBBORN COW

*Read about Steve and Alex's cow. Then write **true** or **false** for the statements on the next page.*

Steve and Alex have a stubborn cow. They try to move their cow. Alex pulls on the rope. Both friends try their best but it does not work. Why doesn't the cow want to walk? Steve and Alex sit and think. They need a better plan. "Moo!" calls the cow. Steve finds some wheat. The cow follows the wheat. It is so hungry.

1. Steve and Alex try to move their cow.

2. Steve pulls on the rope.

3. The cow will not move.

4. Steve and Alex sit and eat.

5. The cow is hungry.

COOKIE TIME FOR STEVE

Read about Steve's cookies. Then fill in the blanks on the next page.

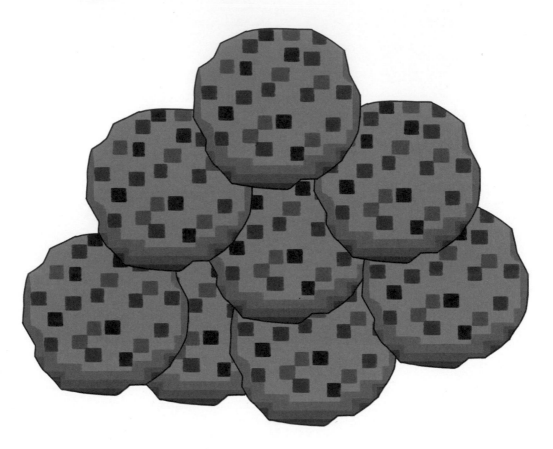

Steve loves to cook! He wants to bake cookies.

Steve finds a crafting recipe. He gathers the

ingredients. He mixes together wheat and cocoa

beans. The recipe makes eight cookies. He can share

the cookies with his friends! Yum! Great job, Steve!

1. Steve wants to bake _____ .

2. Steve finds a crafting _____ .

3. He mixes together

   _____ and cocoa _____ .

4. The recipe makes _____ cookies.

THE SCARY SPIDER

Read about the spider. Then connect the phrases in the left column with the correct answers in the right column.

A spider has a black body and bright red eyes.

It also has eight legs and can climb walls. Spiders

only attack in the night.

Spiders flip onto their

backs when they die.

They can drop string

and a spider eye.

1. A spider has a

        A. red.

2. A spider's eyes are

        B. die.

3. Spiders flip onto their backs when they

        C. black body.

4. A spider can drop

        D. string.

WATCH OUT FOR WITCHES!

Read about the swamp hut. Then use the words in the box to fill in the blanks on the next page.

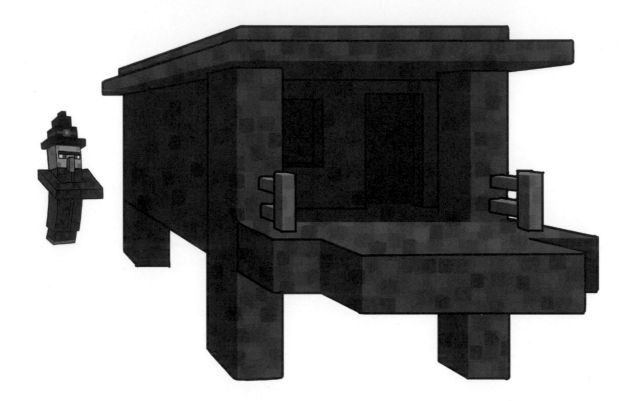

I found a small hut in the swamp. It was made from wood logs. Inside the hut, I saw a flower pot. It had a red mushroom in it! I ran into a black cat. I will tame the cat because I have a raw fish. I hope I do not see a witch next!

Choose from the words below to fill in the blanks.

logs	skeleton	witch	swamp	black
flower	mushroom	because	green	

1. I found a small hut in the _____ .

2. It was made from wood _____ .

3. Inside the hut I saw a _____ pot.

4. It had a red _____ in it!

5. I ran into a _____ cat.

6. I will tame the cat _____ I have a raw fish.

7. I hope I do not see a _____ next!

CRAFTING A BETTER TOOL

Read about Steve's crafting table. Then number the events in the story in the order in which they happened.

Steve needs a stone pickaxe to mine faster.

He does not see a chest, so he will craft his own

pickaxe. First, he finds the recipe. He learns

which items he needs. Next, he gathers three

cobblestones and two sticks. Then, Steve uses a

crafting table to place the stone and sticks in the

grid. Steve makes a stone pickaxe. Finally, Steve

can mine faster!

_____ Steve gathers cobblestones and sticks.

_____ Steve finds the recipe.

_____ Steve can mine faster!

_____ Steve uses a crafting table.

_____ Steve needs a stone pickaxe.

_____ Steve makes a stone pickaxe.

TWO DIFFERENT ANIMALS

Read about a fox and a bat. Then fill in the Venn diagram. Things that are the same about the animals go in the center. Things that are different go on the sides.

A fox sleeps during the day and hunts at night. It runs fast and can jump over walls. A fox eats chickens, rabbits, and fish. A fox has orange or white fur. A fox makes a loud sound in the night.

Bats sleep during the day and hunt at night. They fly around and are found in caves. They fly very fast and can sit or hang on blocks. All bats have black fur and wings. They make a quiet noise.

FOX

BAT

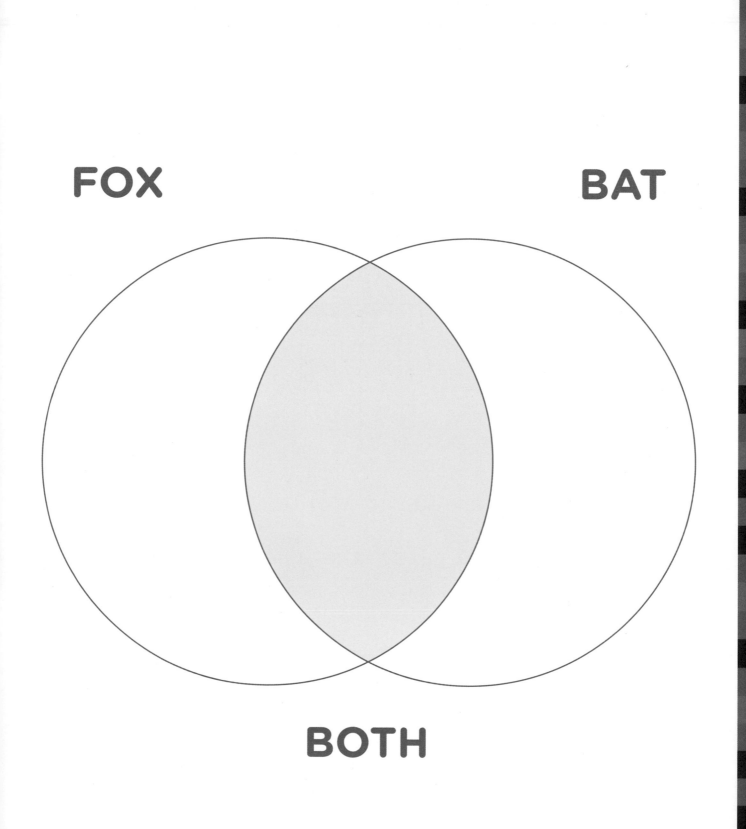

BOTH

IRON GOLEMS

Read about Iron Golems. Then fill in the blanks on the next page.

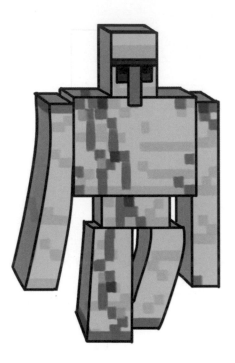

Iron Golems are found around a village and don't move far away from the village houses. Iron Golems are very big and strong. Green plants grow around their body. They are friendly to villagers. An iron golem gives red flowers to villagers as a gift! Iron golems are heavy and sink in water. An Iron Golem uses its long arms to attack. If it is hurt, it will show cracks.

Choose from the words below to fill in the blanks.

strong	stones	friendly	red flowers	legs
village	move	light	arms	heavy

1. An Iron Golem is very big and _____ .

2. Iron Golems are _____ and sink in water.

3. Iron Golems have long _____ .

4. An Iron Golem is _____ to villagers.

5. An iron golem gives _____ to villagers as a gift.

6. Iron Golems are found around a _____ .

7. Iron Golems don't _____ far away from the village houses.

THREE CHEERS FOR SHEARS

Read about shears. Then answer the questions on the next page.

There are many ways to use shears. Shears are the very best tool to use to get wool. A player can cut wool off of a sheep to use for a bed. Shears are also the right tool to make a carved pumpkin mask. This mask can protect a player from an Enderman attack. Finally, if you use shears to cut a beehive, it will drop honey that you can collect in a glass bottle. Shears are a great tool!

1. What is the main idea of this text?

_____

_____

_____

2. Give three details to support the main idea.

DETAIL 1:

_____

_____

_____

DETAIL 2:

_____

_____

_____

DETAIL 3:

_____

_____

_____

ATTACK OF THE GHAST

Read about ghasts. Then answer the questions on the next page.

Alex is in the Nether. Oh no! She sees three ghasts flying above a lava sea. One ghast hears Alex and makes a loud screech sound. They all start to shoot fireballs at her. Fireballs are slow, but they can really hurt you. Alex needs to move. When the ghast closes its eyes, she runs and hides behind a block. If the ghast can't see Alex, the attack will stop. She stays behind the block and waits until the floating mobs leave.

1. *Where* is Alex?

   _____

2. *What* does Alex hear?

   _____

3. *When* does Alex hide behind the block?

   _____

4. *Why* does Alex hide?

   _____

   _____

SLIME'S BEGINNER SIGHT WORDS

Slime is bouncing for joy that you're learning to read. Check off the sight words below as you read them correctly. Keep practicing until you can check all the boxes!

☐ all

☐ as

☐ are

☐ ate

☐ be

☐ by

☐ did

☐ do

☐ eat

☐ four

☐ get

☐ good

☐ now

☐ out

☐ of

☐ saw

☐ say

☐ she

☐ so

☐ soon

☐ that

☐ there

☐ they

☐ what

SKELETON'S SIGHT WORDS POWER LEVEL: 1

Skeletons love hitting their targets, and this skeleton wants you to hit yours. Make it your goal to read each sight word correctly and level up your reading power. Check the box as you learn each word.

- ☐ after
- ☐ again
- ☐ any
- ☐ ask
- ☐ could
- ☐ every
- ☐ fly
- ☐ from
- ☐ give
- ☐ going
- ☐ has
- ☐ her

- ☐ his
- ☐ how
- ☐ know
- ☐ live
- ☐ open
- ☐ over
- ☐ some
- ☐ then
- ☐ walk
- ☐ were
- ☐ when
- ☐ where

STEVE'S SIGHT WORDS POWER LEVEL: 2

Steve uses valuable resources to help him fight mobs and win. Add these sight words to your inventory of skills and you'll have the power you need to face your next reading challenge.

- [ ] always
- [ ] around
- [ ] because
- [ ] been
- [ ] before
- [ ] best
- [ ] both
- [ ] buy
- [ ] call
- [ ] does
- [ ] don't
- [ ] fast
- [ ] first
- [ ] found
- [ ] gave

- [ ] goes
- [ ] made
- [ ] many
- [ ] pull
- [ ] right
- [ ] sleep
- [ ] their
- [ ] these
- [ ] use
- [ ] very
- [ ] which
- [ ] why
- [ ] would
- [ ] write
- [ ] your

1-MINUTE FLUENCY TEST

Have your child read the passage below for exactly one minute. As they read, count the number of words they skip or mispronounce. When the time is up, circle the last word they read and count the total words read. Subtract the number of errors to get their WPM (words per minute) score. Celebrate their success! Repeat the process on another day to see how much they have improved.

Date: _____ WPM: _____

The first day in Minecraft is very fun. You can break blocks and walk around to see the world around you. Maybe you see some trees, some blocks, or some sheep. If you see a tree, you can chop it down to get wood. If you see gray blocks, you can mine them. They are called cobblestone.

Do you hear a hissing sound? That is a creeper. It blows up if you get too close, so stay away! A cat appears and scares the creeper. The creeper turns red and blows up. Get the music disc it drops so you can have a dance party later!

The sky gets dark as you play. You must build a house then make a bed to stay safe. First, you need wool. Find the sheep and get its wool. Use the wood from the tree to make a door and a bed. Time to sleep. You need to rest up for tomorrow. Good night, gamer.

[162 words]

ANSWER KEY

SHORT A (Page 4)

1. B
2. C
3. A
4. E
5. D

SHORT A (Page 5)

1. bat
2. cat
3. hat
4. glass
5. sat

LONG A (Page 6)

1. E
2. C
3. D
4. A
5. B

LONG A (Page 7)

1. cave
2. gate
3. chase
4. hay
5. Strays

SHORT E (Page 8)

1. B
2. A
3. D
4. C
5. E

SHORT E (Page 9)

1. chest
2. gem
3. red
4. wet
5. bed

LONG E (Page 10)

1. B
2. D
3. A
4. E
5. C

LONG E (Page 11)

1. feet
2. green
3. reef
4. sheep
5. tree

SHORT I (Page 12)

1. B
2. E
3. A
4. D
5. C

SHORT I (Page 13)

1. dig
2. fish
3. lit
4. pig
5. flip

LONG I (Page 14)

1. E
2. A
3. D
4. C
5. B

LONG I (Page 15)

1. time
2. fire
3. shine
4. spider
5. mine

SHORT O (Page 16)

1. B
2. D
3. E
4. A
5. C

SHORT O (Page 17)

1. logs
2. pot
3. block
4. rod
5. fox

LONG O (Page 18)

1. A
2. C
3. D
4. E
5. B

LONG O (Page 19)

1. arrow
2. stone
3. boat
4. grow
5. bones

SHORT U (Page 20)

1. B
2. C
3. A
4. E
5. D

SHORT U (Page 21)

1. cut
2. hut
3. sun
4. buzz
5. mud

LONG U (Page 22)

1. D
2. A
3. E
4. C
5. B

LONG U (Page 23)

1. blue
2. suit
3. cube
4. fruit
5. Rubies

SENTENCE BUILDING WITH STEVE (Page 24)

1. C
2. E
3. D
4. A
5. B

PARTS OF A SENTENCE (Page 25)

1. (Piglins) live in the Nether.
2. (They) like gold armor.
3. (Lava) hurts them.
4. (Baby piglins) are passive mobs.
5. (A piglin) becomes a zombie in the Overworld.

MEET ZOMBIFIED PIGLINS (Page 26-27)

1. crimson forest
2. hit
3. Overworld

ALEX AND THE LOOT CHEST (Page 28-29)

1. fast
2. gold bars
3. five
4. tools

HOW TO TAME A LLAMA (Page 30-31)

1. B
2. E
3. A
4. C
5. D

MEET MAGMA CUBES (Page 32-33)

1. jumping
2. smaller cubes
3. one
4. Large cubes jump 4 blocks.
   OR
   Large magma cubes are stronger.

ABANDONED VILLAGES (Page 34-35)

1. False - *Abandoned villages are dirty.*
2. True
3. True
4. False - *Stray cats are found in abandoned villages.*
5. True
6. False - *Zombies can appear there.*

ALEX'S SNOWY WALK (Page 36-37)

1. B
2. A
3. C
4. A
5. B

MEET STRAYS (Page 38-39)

1. cold places
2. bow; arrow
3. spider
4. killed

STEVE AND ALEX'S STUBBORN COW (Page 40-41)

1. True
2. False - *Alex pulls on the rope.*
3. True
4. False - *They sit and think.*
5. True. *It wants to eat the wheat!*

COOKIE TIME FOR STEVE (Page 42-43)

1. cookies
2. recipe
3. wheat; beans
4. eight

THE SCARY SPIDER (Page 44-45)

1. C
2. A
3. B
4. D

WATCH OUT FOR WITCHES! (Page 46-47)

1. swamp
2. logs
3. flower
4. mushroom
5. black
6. because
7. witch

CRAFTING A BETTER TOOL (Page 48-49)

3

2

6

4

1

5

TWO DIFFERENT ANIMALS (Page 50-51)

FOX   **BAT**

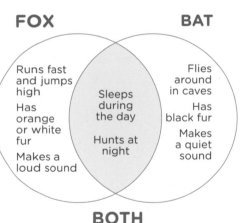

Runs fast and jumps high

Has orange or white fur

Makes a loud sound

Sleeps during the day

Hunts at night

Flies around in caves

Has black fur

Makes a quiet sound

BOTH

IRON GOLEMS (Page 52-53)

1. strong
2. heavy
3. arms
4. friendly
5. red flowers
6. village
7. move

THREE CHEERS FOR SHEARS (Page 54-55)

1. There are many ways to use shears

2. Detail 1:
   Use to get wool
   Detail 2:
   Make a cut pumpkin mask
   Detail 3:
   Cut a beehive for honey

ATTACK OF THE GHAST (Page 56-57)

1. Alex is in the Nether.
2. Alex hears a loud screech sound.
3. When the ghast closes its eyes.
4. So the ghast won't see her and will stop attacking her.